familiars

For Julia + Scott—
Always yours—

familiars

Fol
Chppell

{ poems }

Fred Chappell

Louisiana State University Press

Baton Rouge

Published by Louisiana State University Press
Copyright © 2014 by Fred Chappell
All rights reserved
Manufactured in the United States of America
LSU Paperback Original
First printing

Designer: Laura Roubique Gleason
Typefaces: Minion Pro, text; Livory, display
Printer and binder: Lightning Source

"The Acrophile," "After Hours" (under the title "Midnight"),
"Ambition," "Beside Herself," "Cynosure," "Dark Star," "Emilia
Reveal'd," "For I Will Consider," "Ghost Story" (under the title
of "One Life to Live"), "Hypothecat," "in re reincarnation,"
"Migration," "Passerby," "Presence," "Revival," "Ritual," "Rondo,"
"Second Thoughts," "Security," "Shaftsbury," "Stillness," "The
Burden of History," "Time Piece," "Tom Juan," "Visitor," and
"Window Seat" first appeared in *Companion Volume,* published by
Yonno Press, 2004; "Cousin Marjorie," "Perseverance," and "Uncle
John" first appeared in *Family Gathering,* published by Louisiana
State University Press, 1995. "Difference" and *"The Animals of
Heaven"* are forthcoming in *North Carolina Literary Review;*
"White Out" is forthcoming in *Sewannee Review.*

LIBRARY OF CONGRESS CATALOGING-IN-PUBLICATION DATA
Chappell, Fred, 1936–
  [Poems. Selections]
  Familiars : poems / Fred Chappell.
    pages ; cm
  ISBN 978-0-8071-5749-7 (pbk. : alk. paper) —
  ISBN 978-0-8071-5750-3 (pdf) — ISBN 978-0-8071-5751-0 (epub) —
  ISBN 978-0-8071-5752-7 (mobi)
  I. Title.
  PS3553.H298A6 2014
  811'.54—dc23
                                                    2014005811

Dedicated to

Dr. Christine E. Hunt

Healer   Consoler   Innovator

Contents

Introductory

In 2000, the poetry collection *Family Gathering* appeared, a portrait gallery of the members of a fictional southern clan. About a year later, Susan and I were conversing with our friend, the fine paper artist Susanne Martin, when our two longhairs, Chloe and Marti, entered the room. Susanne was describing some of the kinds of material from which she made paper. Susan said, "Too bad you can't make paper out of cat hair. We have an abundance."

"Oh but I can," said Susanne.

Thus was born the notion of *Companion Volume,* which was to be a portrait gallery of the cats belonging to the personages sketched in *Gathering. Companion Volume* came out in 2004 in a limited edition of fifty copies, the paper made of feline combings, the poems printed on the flatbed press of Susanne's Yonno Press in Greensboro, North Carolina. This book was illustrated with elegant wit and panache by the celebrated Viennese artist Fritz Janschka.

That edition is long out of print.

Yet the original concept was not carried out. As I composed the poems, I soon discovered that the cats I sought to bring into the compass of the concept did not often cotton to the personages I had limned in the earlier book. They were an independent lot, preferring to keep company with humans of their own choosing or to maintain their individuality as solitaries. In the end, only Aunt Muriel, Cousin Lilias, Cousin Marjorie, Uncle John, and Morris the Chair were able to attract purring friends. The other cats pursued their own destinies.

For that reason, the title *Companion Volume* has proved misleading. This present collection, *Familiars,* includes only four poems from *Family Gathering,* and only twenty-one from the limited edition, mostly in different forms, reworked and retitled. All the rest are new acquaintances, perhaps drawn to my writing desk by the sound of scribbling, which to them may suggest mouse-work.

This collection of homages to the felines had perforce to include proper salutes to other celebrators whose work has provided inspiration for many years. "Time Piece" is an imagined scenario for a strip of George Herriman's genius *Krazy Kat;* "in re reincarnation" brings back Don Marquis's immortals, archy the cockroach and mehitabel; "Jubilate Felis" is a salute to "For I will consider my cat Geoffrey" from Christopher Smart's *Jubilate Agno;* and "Recognition" is an adaptation from Baudelaire's "Le chat, II."

I am proud to acknowledge my deep gratitude to Porter and Fritz Janschka, Susanne and John Martin, and to Susan Nicholls Chappell. Our friends at debjessehall@aol.com have provided invaluable technical support.

> *Let Cecilia choir with Iris and exalted Aurora*
> For Susan outshines the Rainbows of Eternity.

familiars

Difference

How powerful a presence is her absence.
No Sheba naps, curled on the counterpane,
Or sits at the casement to memorize the rain,
Or tussles with the tassels of a valance
With tigress energy and unsheathed talons,
Or attends with steady gaze the calm routine
Of household duties droning round again
From her vigilant bookshelf eminence.

The armchair is not empty but incomplete
And the patch of sunlit rug unoccupied
More vacant than the sky when the moon is hid
In the cavern of December's longest night.

These rooms were quiet when she was resident.
Now they lie silent. That is different.

Cynosure

Reginald's a sartorial wonder
With his coat of powder gray, his stockings white
And of an even height.
Sitting on his tuffet with his paws tucked under,
He's a striking sight.

But he holds no position in any house.
He will not deign to notice a mouse;
His *grand seigneur* demeanor
Suggests the domicile might be cleaner;
His imperturbable *sang froid*
Causes most to feel irreclaimably bourgeois
And no decorator can hatch up
Ways for the ambience to match up.

Hollywood shows interest now and then;
They call him out, then ship him back again,
For in his noble presence
Even billionaire actors
And arrogant directors
Come off like peasants.

Try to avoid his ownership;
Keep well afar.
You'll only wind up in the grip
Of crushing debt for caviar.
You'll never gain his gratitude.

That ain't Reginald's attitude.

Beatitude

If thoughtful Marian gets her wish,
She'll never eat another fish
And will immediately scram
When offered a repast of ham;
She will never make a meal
Of pork or venison or veal
And will turn away her eyes
From toothsome steak and kidney pies,
Regarding all such fare as carrion.

The fine ambition of our Marian
Is to become a vegetarian
And when she can accomplish that
She'll be a most accomplished cat,
Savoring cabbage, beets, and kale
With a sturdy India ale,
Embracing the regimen of Cato
And the homely, solemn potato,
Praising the spirit of the rutabaga,
Though other felines think her gaga.

She'll arch her back and preen her fur
When the Dalai Lama blesses her,
And all the rodents will cease their plaint
And adore our Marian as their Saint.

Emilia Reveal'd

Emilia flows into the room
With such confident majesty
That all admire her calm aplomb
And unforbidding gravity.

She acknowledges but does not fawn;
She does not leap upon a lap
That does not wish to be leapt upon;
She's graceful even when savoring a nap.

She does not sprinkle the rug with hairs
Better left in other places;
She does not claw upholstered chairs
Into hideous disgraces.

She keeps herself immaculate
With careful grooming head to tail;
She so enjoys being a cat
That she insists on doing it well.

No one affronts her dignity
With crude remarks or obscene jokes;
She charms the ill-bred family
Into being polished folks.

Yet if the moon is shining bright
Into neighbor Smith's backyard
Where glowing roses perfume the site,
Emilia may let down her guard

And caper about, coming unglued,
Alarming the judgmental owl
When joined by a kink-tail biker dude
Who matches her pleasures yowl for yowl.

Then she appears the following day
With every whisker combed just right,
Unrumpled, cool, as if to say,
"Who were those dreadful cats last night?"

Migration

Finally the moted sunlight
Marti has followed across the rug
This February afternoon,
Napping in its glow all snug
And cozy, diminishes to dun light,
Then darkens like a tarnishing spoon.

So she seeks out the register
Where the furnace breathes into the room
An arid, fumy pour of air
That now within the sunless gloom
Makes a tropic of her fur.

She plumps herself into bolster form
And shuts her eyes and curls her paws
And sinks into an opium doze
That causes her to feel twice warm
As we advance, listless and weary,
Through this endless February.

Security

Paisano knows the farm like no one else;
As he patrols the farms, the fields, the pasture,
Nothing escapes his gaze. You may cast your
Eye from saw-tooth hills to nestling dells,
But you won't see a tenth of what he sees,
Down among the beetles and the bees.

He's got a cast-iron schedule that he follows:
First to the milking shed to catch a squirt,
And then to take a roll in cow-lot dirt,
And then to give his newborn offspring solace;
For while the mother forages for food,
He teaches games that train for tomcathood.

And then the landscape beckons with green finger:
He's off to search the haystack where field mice
Have built apartment houses more than twice;
Then by the peaceful creek bank he will linger,
Debating whether to find his fishing pole
And bathe a worm or two in his lucky hole.

On to the sty where the hogs are snuffling slops;
Then to the stable to hear as Jackson and Maude
Discuss good-naturedly the idea of God,
Their tranquil argument that never stops.
He listens carefully, for both these mules
Trace out a logic that could confound the schools.

His favorite napping spots include the grove
Of oaks above the farther barn, a patch
Of sassafras below, a dusky thatch
Of secret ivy. In between he'll rove
As far abroad as Wilson's dog-run fence,
Though very quickly he returns from thence.

He notes the flights of swallows, songs of wrens;
He counts the robins, bobwhite, and the quail,
Admires the rainbow of the rooster's tail,
Alert for any sound disturbing the hens.
The fox and weasel do not despoil and rob;
The farm is safe. Paisano's on the job.

Shaftesbury

You've heard him howl when they did murder Caesar;
You've watched him try to solace mad King Lear;
In *A Christmas Carol* he disdains Ebenezer,
Then curls around the crutch of Tiny Tim;
He was the special pet of Professor 'Iggins;
Caroused with Falstaff when the foaming piggins
Went round and round again in malty cheer.
Many a younger player looked up to him
As the finest second lead upon the stage.

But now the scenes have changed. On television
He hawks Kleen Kitty litter and flea collars,
Bowing to his agent's gruff decision.
I understand a chap must gather dollars—
But this is the saddest scandal of our age!

Cousin Marjorie

Oh when she's there she's so immensely there
No color but her own, no voice but hers,
No other nature can advance itself;
She is the noontime that absorbs the day-moon.

Large in every sense, rich, overblown,
Rose that droops from surfeit of itself;
Bright flowing dresses brave as carnival bunting:
All Marjorie's grand Everything is here.

The dimpled hands, the sensual smile, the stare
That takes you in as warmly as a perfume,
All sympathy and calm attentiveness:
So much herself it seems she has no self

But only Presence that if taken away
Would cause such lessening of the sense of place
You'd think the room was now no more itself
But only a diminished facsimile:

A room wherein a chamber symphony
Played Schubert for an hour and then departed,
The chairs left emptier than before they came,
So much herself she is wild Selflessness,

Has no more concept of a Marjorie
Than has a waterfall, a sunbaked stone,
The dew-strung spider thread, the snuffling spaniel,
The rain-wet sweet gum spread-armed in City Park.

The Elect

The brindle cat named Rogue resides
With Marjorie, her six canaries,
Her brash and thoughtless Scottie pup,
And her unassuming terrapin.

They're all in love with her. How not?
She is the universe that mantles
Their universes. She is the center
That cuddles all their boundaries.

And each of them believes that she
Adores it more than all the rest
And that someday she'll rid herself
Of the rude, extraneous, useless others

And dedicate her whole existence
To it alone. The songsters hold
This faith, and Tim the terrapin,
And Tam the dog, and Rogue the brindle cat.

Inconceivable to each
Of them that it will not belong
To the sainted elect and, haloed, stand
On the right-hand side of Marjorie

Forever and ever and ever and ever.

Second Thoughts; or,
As You Like It

When his housecat overturned the ink
And marched apace across the immortal pages
Recording Arden Forest's tuneful woodnotes
And Jaques' speech on mankind's seven ages,
The bard decided he must rethink,
     Heigh-ho the wind and the rain!
       And do them all again.

Pay no attention to what the Baconian says:
It was the man Shakespeare who wrote the plays,
While his cat Bardolph contributed the footnotes.

The Burden of History

His chronicle of the human race
Having advanced to Volume Ten—
One thousand unwritten pages each—
Aelius decides he'll need more space
Merely to bring it up to when
The species was ready to be taught
The lore that felines were sent to teach
This backward and uncultured strain.

He looks toward 3000 b.c.
When civilization greets its dawn;
In Egypt the cat's ascendancy
Into the imposing pantheon
Of monumental gods at last is
Accomplished with divine Bubastis.

From there on out, it's evident
The feline's dominance of history
Is almost absolute, though now
And then you'll find a century
When the light of reason is nearly spent
And the heathen worship the god Bow Wow.

That's in the future. First, he must deal with
The hide-clad, lousy, ignorant bunch
No respected cat would take a meal with,
Not even an impromptu lunch.

His friends ask why he wastes his mind
Rehearsing the story of this breed
Distinguished only by fear and greed,
The species always eons behind
The evolutionary curve.
Why give them better than they deserve?
He does not answer. The truth is that
He feels compassion for their need—
And compassion's shameful in a cat.

in re reincarnation

boss it s happened
again   this time a slick
talking tom with less than
honorable
intentions has pulled
the old reincarnation stuff
telling mehitabel not only
was she cleopatra
but also marie antoinette
in her former lives and
catherine the great
and elizabeth one and edna st
vincent millay and mata
hari   next it will be
joan of arc
and you know how this guff
hoodoos her   i said
this world needs no more
former cleopatras
and certainly no more
single parent kittens
but she huffed up
and stalked off and later
i heard them singing
from the fish
cannery roof this duet

                    he
o you were queen of the nile
and i was your trembling slave
when you ruled the tropic isle
i was a lowly knave

i ve worshiped you from afar
while all the ages rolled
for a thousand thousand eons
our story will be told

she

o rise and do not grovel
on your knees before me
no more the oar and shovel
will be your destiny

i raise thee to the rank of prince
and grant thee a coronet
and we shall revel since
there s a dance in the old dame yet

then as says the bard
the rest was silence
i tell you boss this
time she has lost
her mind completely
i m thinking in a former
life she must have been one of those cats
who believed she was cleopatra
in a former life and
so on

Paperweight

Ramses, carved from African blackwood,
Lies on the cluttered desk to depress the flood
Of learned correspondence and student theme.

His posture takes the noble attitude
Of desert Sphinxes in their vast solitude
Who seal themselves within an endless dream.

This figure removed from Time and its distress
Befriends Professor Osgood's loneliness
As wearily he tends his midnight flame.

The hour sifts away. The neighborhood
Is sleeping. Lamp off . . . He goes to find his bed.
The immeasurable trance of *Ramses* fills the room

And enters all the shadow of the house,
Bearing visions of ancient images,
Of every journeying pharaoh in his tomb,

Lying in golden state, accompanied
By a chosen feline, likewise mummified,
To search out pathways through eternal gloom.

Ghost Story

What does Alexander see,
Staring with taut fixity
Into the dusty corner there
And its eerily vacant air?

Perhaps invisible Somethings flock
That barren angle of the room
And speak to him at twelve o'clock
Of an unalterable doom.

It would not be a single ghost
But several who gaze and wait
Until the Halloween veils with frost
The leaf-strewn lawn, the gray roof-slate,

To whisper to him in unison
The dreaded sentence that constrains
Him to a destiny fordone:
"Us eight you squandered. *One remains.*"

Cousin Lilias

Within a shadow dark with murmur, wise
As midnight, Cousin Lilias slides, footfalls
Noiseless as spiders' thought. Her amber eyes
Are slow and watchful, as if she hunts for prey.
She seems to move in time to a bell that tolls
Beyond the ordered measures of night and day,
Her mind a prospect of indifferent skies.

No one talks with her. The family
Falls quiet when at times her velvet presence
Is noticed in the room. What did she see?
What does she know? She is the palpable essence
Of something they cannot name, a mystery
Defying each solution they invent,
A troubling omen that the future sent.

Their desperate theories remain inadequate.
Cousin Lilias is not the Cousin Lilias
She used to be. She has become of late
A kind of figure they can never know,
Still unnerving, cold and supercilious—
But now the puppet of her Alter Ego,
The superbly evil Grimoire, her cat.

Genius Loci

Cousin Lilias never comprehends
She is subservient to the confident creature
Who pads from living room to bedroom, blends
His shadow with the shadow of the bookcase,
The leather chair, the somber drapes. His nature
Becomes one with the house as daylight ends:
Grimoire is *the genius of the place:*

A place that Lilias's former lovers found
Disquieting when the ominous night
Folded its implacable silence around
The cozy banalities of the neighborhood,
Altered the mellow glow of the porch light,
Deepened the creeping darkness across the ground
Where the grass snake hunted and the red oak stood.

No suitor ever earned Grimoire's approval;
Each of them was guilty of some deed
That warranted a swift and clean removal,
Although none of them became aware
Of the ungracious thing he did or said
That made our Lilias so diligent with a shovel.

Grimoire's chart marks where the bodies are.

Recognition

One time only I stroked his fur
Streaked brown and gold, and there arose
A sweet musk powerful and close,
A soft, embalming atmosphere.

He is the genius loci here,
To judge, to order, inspire and guide
All things soever in his empire.
Is he a Fairy King? A god?

When I observe this cherished being
That draws, as a lover would, my gaze,
I see within his eyes my eyes,
In his seeing my own seeing;

And find, amazed, a glowing fire
Intense within his pale pupils,
Penetrant rays of living opals.
They hold me fixed in his calm stare.

—after Baudelaire

Passerby

Black Margo stalks across a grave,
Casting her moonlit shadow on the name
Of the tenant peaceful beneath the stone
In his bony frame.

Does Someone call him forth to stand
More naked than the day that he was born,
Upon the right or the left hand
In triumph or scorn?

He cannot know. He only feels
That gentle touch of old mortality
Purfle the surface of his sleep
As she slides by.

Then he descends once more those depths
Wherein the darkness tides its silence over
The clay of every fallen warrior
And fallen lover.

Black Margo, ever unaware,
Explores a farther length of moon-bleached lawn,
Brushing with umbra another name
On another stone.

Uncle John

One may say of Uncle John he's *there,*
But not that "there" is changed by this cool fact.
He's not invisible, the way that air
And metaphysics are. He'll speak and act,
As other people do, and yet he's seen
But hardly noticed, like a nondescript
Monument amid excited children
Playing in the park at green twilight.

The thought has been advanced that Uncle John
Should not be counted with the human race
But rather as a separate phenomenon,
An extensive quality of physical space,
Like *length* and *width* and *depth,* a whole dimension
Unto himself unmarked . . . Contrariwise,
Some claim such blandness is his sly intention,
That he's perfected a helluva good disguise.

If you believe in spooks, then Uncle John
May fit your definition—unless you find
That he's too incorporeal for one,
Making such slight impression on the mind
That he'd be snubbed by any proper ghost.
And yet I've wondered if that's not his plan:
In mortal flesh he lives as a specter lost,
So when he dies he'll come back as a man.

Hypothecat

Let us try to imagine that Uncle John
Might have a cat and that this animal
Was so well suited to the tenuous man
That it would own no other host at all.
Let us further premise that it possessed
A sixth or seventh necessary sense
That could perceive our uncle and attest
That to the "there" he made some difference.

What sort of creature would it have to be?
We must resort to pure hypothesis,
Deducing with a stringent theory
The probable nature of its properties:
It won't be strokable or teasable;
It eats no food and it pursues no mouse;
It has no smell and is invisible
And occupies no space in Uncle's house.

How then can we honestly define
This immaterial concept as a cat?
We must establish a taxonomic line,
Distinguishing *which* from *what* and *this* from *that,*
And list our cats together on one side,
Insist that they be made of flesh and bone,
With fur and purr and claw and paw and hide—
Or else they'll all end up like Uncle John.

After Hours

Midnight in the main branch library,
The hour when Nora makes her faithful rounds,
Tasting smells, investigating sounds
That could mean threats to the security
Of the stiff wisdom of laborious sages
Who sputtered ink on all these frowsty pages.

She's velvet black and melts into the blacks
That lie in oblongs on the lobby floor,
Thrown by streetlight through the windowed door.
They pave the way to the darkness of the stacks
Wherein she enters now with stealthy tread
Among the dog-eared Read and crisp Unread.

Mute voices surround her in the night:
Merry prattle of nursery rhymes, stentorian
Periods of moralist and historian,
Novelists who titillate or affright,
Athletes boasting of everything they do,
Poets for fit audience though few.

Such noise she barely heeds. Her duty is
To listen for the near inaudible swish
And skitter of mouse, beetle, and silverfish,
The mutter of computer viruses
And other foes of books whose keenest joy
Is singling out intelligence to destroy.

Her itinerary takes her down the stair
Out of General Circulation into
The narrow aisles where visitors are few,
Past Maps and Special Collections where
The Founder's letters slumber in a box,
And the labyrinthine mazes of GovDocs.

At last her tour concludes and now she finds
In the dark farthest corner her special nook
Where she relaxes to peruse a book
And socialize with famous brilliant minds
That every cat feels privileged to know:
Sherlock, Maigret, Lord Wimsey, and Poirot.

Evening Watch

Moonrise we march to the village square,
Berta, Tully, Bandy, and I,
And sit in a ring round the gibbet where
Our mistress Hulga was made to die.
We observe in silence the empty air
Until the moon claims all the sky.

Then we return to her tumbled hut
To slay the rat that gnaws the rind,
To fend the hateful adder out
And call the peaceful days to mind;
For whether she were witch or not,
Only Hulga ever was kind.

Visitor

Chloe slips into Susan's dream
And, though she hunts most thoroughly,
Can find no Stilton, crickets, or cream,
But only a mouseless penury
That makes her wonder once again
Why humans have such reputation
For possessing a superior brain
And brighter imagination.

There's nothing here but flower beds
In predictable order, apple-pie;
Among these yellows and warm reds
Floats but a single butterfly.
A mockingbird sits in a beech,
Caroling full-throated joy,
Grandly, proudly out of reach
Purposely to annoy Chloe—

Or so it seems to the tortoise shell
Who now decides to leave behind
The bland and ultra-pleasant hell
Of Susan's sweetly pastoral mind
And investigate the dream of Fred
As he lies shivering in its power
On the sweaty side of the conjugal bed
In his troubled midnight hour.

She slowly approaches this moiling mind,
Toxic as a plug of tobacco,
And like no other she might find:
8/10 s oatmeal, 2/10 s wacko.
Then once again Chloe retreats,
Happy to escape so handily
This phantasmagoria she meets
That tests her stalwart sanity.

She seeks her accustomed place
At the pedal end of the counterpane,
Strongly determined that she will pace
The dreams of Susan never again.
The blood-cloud-fire nightmare of Fred
She shall repress as best she can
With all its fury of doom and dread—
What a dolefully peculiar man!

Pillow Talk

Cousin Deddle never sleeps alone
    To lie vulnerable
While the window fills up with moon
    And his soul with trouble.

Brindle Melinda shares his tousled bed,
    Watching as he dreams
Of the embittered, guilty dead
    Going up in flames.

She listens as each night he murmurs
    Darker phrases than he should,
Feverish truths she always remembers.

    Oh . . . This can't be good.

Ritual

Do you vow by existence One
Never to utter the secret name
Of any feline wild or tame
Either in earnest or in fun?

I so vow.

Do you vow by existence Two
To give no quarter to any mouse
You find a-field or in the house,
No matter how it pleads with you?

I so vow.

Do you vow by existence Three
To live a life of cleanliness,
To sharpen your claws and wash your face
And lick your fur fastidiously?

I so vow.

Do you vow by existence Four
To hold in closest secrecy
Our role in human history
And our books of forbidden lore?

I so vow.

Do you vow by number Five
Not to reveal our dialect
To any human intellect
As long as ever you shall live?

I so vow.

Do you vow by existence Six
To propagate the feline species
According to our Maker's wishes
And never with dogs to intermix?

I so vow.

Do you vow by number Seven
To find a special hiding place
You can retire to just in case
Of sudden need for a safe haven?

I so vow.

Do you vow by number Eight
That you will skillfully improvise
A music like an infant's cries
To accompany when you mate?

I so vow.

Will you vow by the final Nine
To honor our elder divinities
Bringing sacrifice to these
When you visit the ancient shrine?

I so vow.

By our hereditary right
Performed upon this springtime night
With symbolic feast of rat
Celebrated by moonlight:

No longer kitten—you are Cat.

Perseverance

Aunt Muriel is the belle that rings forever.
She must count seven decades anyhow,
Yet still maintains the airs of a glamour-puss
Of twenty-two. The years cannot dissever
Her graces from her. She makes a charming fuss
Over petty trifles. The men still scrape and bow,

She being the sexiest woman in the room.
Her face is lined but keeps its fine profile;
She lights a cigarette with cool finesse,
The naughty thing. She flashes a winning smile
And speaks in a gin contralto that seals our doom:
"This old rag? I'd hardly call it a *dress*—"

She acknowledges the compliments she draws
With practiced ease and prattles without stop,
Breathily breathless, silken as liquid soap.
She seems always to bow to silent applause.
We see through her but love her still because,
By the living God Who made her, she gives us hope.

Rival

But Babydoll is hip to all these ploys
She's seen Aunt Muriel work ten thousand times:
She knows that business with the cigarette;
She's heard the woolen whisper of that voice;
She's watched the gentlemen flare up in flames
From the fuse the dear old arsonist has lit.

It's all mere flummery, thinks Babydoll,
A childish game that silly humans play
As they weave round the warped Maypole of sex.
They show, these rubes, no dignity at all,
And as for *beauty,* no one can gainsay
The superior graces of a Devon Rex—

Which, as it happens, is what Babydoll is.
As if to prove her point, she steps out
Into the room, purring her warmest purr,
Displaying the supple tail she flexes about
To emphasize her suave felicities.
Aunt Muriel smokes—but everyone watches *her.*

Tom Juan

Laboring to impress the young soprano,
First he takes her to the Rainbow Room
Where Oscar Felison ripples the piano.
           She drinks Black Satins,
           He Manhattans,
And reveals the latest scandals and points out who's with whom.

Afterward they dine at Le Trianon:
           Vichyssoise,
             Salmon en croûte,
       Endive salade with kiwi fruit,
       Crème brûleé with a touch of framboise.
       Mon Dieu, he really lays it on.
They talk excitedly about the newest show,
       Dispatching a bottle of Veuve Cliquot.

And then they're off to a special place
       To dance until the sun
Opens his bloodshot eye and shows his grumpy face.
       Then, just at break of dawn,
       When the world is nimble with spring
       And Tom is feeling bolder
     They retreat into the garden to sing
The love duet of Tristan and Isolde.

But these are star-crossed singers, fated
To suffer contumely and scorn;
Their music is underappreciated.
They're uninvited to sing at the Met,
       Their ambitions lie forlorn . . .

       And yet—
     Look at the reviews
       They get:
Two dozen mismatched pairs of shoes,
Eight Patterson novels, a child's tea set,

Cracked coffee pots of various hues,
A delicious hamster that recently died,
A dented flugelhorn . . .

I know poets who'd be satisfied.

Jubilate Felis

Let cherub Angels sound Rejoicement upon keen trumpets.
For I will consider my Mistress Susan.

Let praise that cometh from the heart be ever a Balm.
For when she calls me Pretty Chloe and Darling Chloe soft light
magnetic shines in her face.

Let anger be a Black Tiger never to be countenanced.
For when she calls me other names not nice she does not intend
them & is only in a roaring Pet.

Let Obadiah play upon the Lute and hearken.
For when she consoles herself by combing me she will sing and
murmur and accompany with her thumb on the comb.

Let Seraphim rise to the prismic Apex of heaven.
For the clouds of my combed hair are most wondrous.

For she will watch a Television machine with birds of interest in-
side the belly of it.

For I will lie upon her lap and observe the television birds also.

For when she stabs me with the Giant Needle and mutters Irrigate
she believes it a kindness.

Let all Nature converse each in her tongue.
For she speaks to me friendly tho' still she has not learned the lan-
guage.

For she will nuzzle me for joy.

Let Bast rejoice with Kibbles in the Day to Come.
For she offers me a variety of viands to exercise my gourmandise &
extend it widely.

For she does not know what I am laughing about.

For she is mostly peaceful when asleep.

For she is soft to nudge and to knead.

For she lays out rugs of many colors to stretch and prank upon and rub, tho' she believes I cannot tell the colors.

For her naïveté is charming in many regards.

> Let all creatures share the Epiphany that grows in the yard outside.

For she knows what Cat Nip does but not what it is.

For when she treads upon my tail she is much in sorrow and makes apology of abjection and in Reality.

For she does not treat my sister Marti as sweetly as she treats me.

For she knows that a Black cat does not deserve such treatment and is a parvenu.

For she understands that intelligence is rarely conferred upon black cats.

> Let Ebenezer attend that Justice may be delivered in due and proper Course.

For someday she will send Marti away to the Place of Black Cats distant and barren.

For she is not so graceful as a cat. —Poor Susan! Thou hast bled thy hand with the giant Needle.

For she is not subtle and shows evidences of scheming.

For at morning I will dance and sing about the kitchen table and she will look and in time reward my performance.

For she is forced to eat Repulsive food. —Poor Susan! No Tender Vittles comes to thy bowl.

For the glow of her nimbus is electrical and pleasing.

For she will read instructive books not beneficial to eyesight.

> *Let David on his Harp praise bourbon for its friendship and warmth.*

For she can soothe Loudlubber when he is weighty.

For Loudlubber has stolen a chant from Christopher Smart who was a mighty Kit and she must flatter him often.

For she allows me crickets surprising and agile when they are in season and numerous.

For she takes up my Regurgitation in white paper and disappears it.

For she is known among women as blonde as I am known among cats as blonde, tho' I am blonder than she in many ways.

> *Let the Mountain Tops ring with my name and a few others.*

For she tells other women Chloe is a good cat that they may advance to remark and confirm.

For she is not jealous though having noted my greater excellences.

For she brings in dusty Gravel that I may gladden it with my Piss.

For all her hair is upon her head and gives her stomach no protection. —Poor Susan! Thou must remain bald of belly!

For though she cannot sing in the proper way as I do she can Hum.

For the magnetic of her is tuneful.

For she knows she is Susan but does not know how.

For she knows I am Chloe but does not know why.

Let the majesty of Chloe be saluted with much Hallelujah.
For such is the Kingdom of Heaven.

Portals

Minos guards the door to Basement Hell
Where scores of disenfranchised veterans dwell:
Moth-eaten woolens and de-handled jugs
Find space among wolf spiders and dead bugs;
Bundled newsprint grimy, odorous, damp
Slumbers beside a mutilated lamp;
The broken flower pot and watering can
Await the advent of the garbage man.
A dragon in the center belches fumes
That viaduct into the upstairs rooms
Where the plastic Santa never may show his face.
Minos keeps such things in proper place.

The rush of mighty waters, the steamy heat
Of monsoon wilderness, the pulsing beat
Of primitive song within the shower stall:
Sheena's spirit vibrates to the call
Of daybreak jungle. Beside the bathroom door
She crouches like a tiger, alert for
Any opportunity to find
A way into the Place that claims her mind.
But now the smell of new-washed human creature
Despoils her reverie of unspoiled Nature.
The barricade swings open to reveal
A sterile desert of porcelain and tile.

Enrico supplicates the attic door.
Hour on hour he sits devout before
The unresponsive pine in certitude
The universe behind the passive wood
Differs from all that any cat has known,
A world where seas of cream obey a moon
Composed of costly cheeses delectable,
Where catnip is the only vegetable

The fortunate ecology allows;
The only animals felines, birds, and cows.
Someday this door will open. His steadfast faith
Comforts *Enrico* until his dying breath.

Beside   Herself

Chloe I finds Chloe II
dimensionless and untrue,
odorless, silent, totally ersatz,
not a bit like other cats.
Nothing about her is creative;
even her stare is imitative;
all her physical messages are
ones First Chloe transmitted before.
She noses the face to inquire the name;
the other Chloe responds the same.
An insolent glance, designed to annoy,
is faithfully mocked by Second Chloe.
She raises a paw as if to strike
and Chloe II threatens alike.
This game is stupid, she decides,
then turns her back, disdainfully glides
toward the exit away from the peerer
who's safe inside the door-length mirror.
She hoists her tail in a parting taunt:
some cats have got it *and some cats don't.*

The Navigator

Anselm desires to cross the street
To a neighbor porch where a bowl of treat
He daily enjoys has been set out.
Here's the problem: It rained last night;
The forward route is plagued with wet.
Icy puddles threaten his feet.

Now his inherent distaste for water
Requires that he must chart a course
Untried and perilous, to traverse
The road without a jot of spatter,
Drip, or splash, or liquidous worse.

But he misjudges and sets his paw
In a patch he thought as dry as straw
But is in fact quite the reverse.

We live in a treacherous universe.

Motley

"A thing of rags and patches":
Motley loved to romp
Among the autumn leaves,
To tumble, wallow, plump
With a triumphant leap
Into a yellow, brown,
Scarlet, and ochre heap,
And scatter the colorful caches
Across a fresh-combed lawn.

With markings black and dun,
Carrot red and powder gray,
He seemed an effect of sun
Within a windy day
Where the ensemble of his colors
Mirrored his universe.

In him the season found
Means to display its soul.
Dancing a dervish round,
He personified the whole
Carnival of his time:
The maples' red parade,
The willow leaves gone lime,
The fern's cinnamon frond,
The oak-grove harlequinade.

And as the carnival passed,
He joined that company,
Departing with a last
Frisking of paw and tail,
Saluting the bitter chill,
The dark November wind,
That brought the gaiety
Of October to its end.

Winter he would not abide;
That landscape stark and bare
Offered no place to hide
In camouflage, to peek
And spy on the unaware;
There is no motley there.

No Motley anywhere.

Snowflake

As her name would indicate,
It seemed she could appear
Out of the wintry air,
Tiny, delicate, white,
A moment suspended there,
Then dropping without sound
Upon the muddy ground.

She trembled like a mouse
Foreseeing an early death.
Light as a wisp of hay,
She might be blown away
As by a puff of breath
In the early April day
As rowdy winds arose.

Could bright Snowflake survive?
Some things that exist,
Too exquisite to live,
Vanish like the mist
Enwreathing a daybreak grove;
And will not, cannot, stay.
Noontime burns it away.

The things that she must learn
She had to teach herself:
To imitate the wolf
And avoid the losing fight;
In the moonlit, feral night
Lie silent as a log;
Stand confident and stern
To face down any dog;
To feint, recoil, and leap,
And schedule regular sleep.

Now in the tall June grass,
In the annual Feline Games
That glorify the summer,
She challenges every comer
And, as the Games progress
Beneath the solstice sun,
Defeats them one by one,
And on a plaque of brass
Inscribes the record down.

Thus has it come to pass:
Little Snowflake is taking names
And kicking ass.

The Artful Dodger Out of the Bag

Interviewer: *So many have heard of your Great Escape,*
The way you survived to lend us hope,
They clamor to hear your true Life Story.
Were you always destined for Glory?

Glory, you say? We didn't know any.
We lived in a shameful poverty.
Old Man decided that we were too many
And desired us sunken to the bottom of the sea.

"Old Woman," he said, "bag up them cats.
Snivel and bawl, I don't give a durn.
It's all we can do to feed our own brats.
They're headed for the River of No Return."

"But William," said she, "don't be unkind.
They're oh so funny and oh so cute.
I'll share with them, I really won't mind."
The Old Man said, "I don't give a hoot."

She pleaded, she wailed, she begged, and she cried,
But Old Man's heart was hard as a rock.
When she tried to appeal to his merciful side
He drew back his fist and gave her a knock.

So we knew what was up and we scattered away,
Three under the bed and two in a shelf.
She couldn't catch any, try as she may.
"You're useless," says he, "I'll do it myself."

He came at us now with his big clumsy hands.
We made ourselves small and cowered in fear.
He overturned tables and candle-stands,
He busted the mug from which he swilled beer.

I laughed so hard I was helpless as soup
To watch the Old Man fumble and blunder;
The cabinet fell, it knocked him for a loop;
He dropped to the floor with a thump like thunder.

The Old Woman ran to help him arise,
And I went to gloat on him took down a peg,
But when I got there he opened his eyes,
And reached out and grabbed my right hind leg.

Into the burlap, spitting and yowling;
Out of the house and into the lane.
I decided right then to give up my howling
And try if I could employ my brain.

I unsheathed a claw, one single claw,
And severed the sack-threads one by one,
Thinking to free my right front paw
By the time we reached the deep mill-run.

We got to the water just before dark.
The Old Man stood on the bank of grass
And said to the world, "This is Wholesome Work,"
When I extended around and tattered his ass.

He let go the totesack and grabbed at his butt;
He yelled Blue Murder, a hair-raising screech.
When the sack touched the ground I squirmed right out,
Nimble to keep just out of his reach.

He leapt at me twice and then once again;
I was dodging along the brink of the mill-race;
When he lunged the last time he went over and in,
Receiving his baptism with surly ill grace.

He splashed and he thrashed and he kept going down;
It looked like he'd met a well-deserved doom;
But then with a shout that alarmed the whole town,
He managed to grapple the lip of the flume.

When he pulled himself out I made tracks for home
To warn my sisters the Old Man was coming;
Drenched from his boot soles plumb to his dome,
Wild as a cockfight, he'd be cussing and fuming.

He banged through the door and stood in a daze;
He opened his mouth but no word sounded.
She looks him all over and the Old Woman says,
"Appears like you was the one that got drowneded."

Interviewer. *Your heroic exploits inspire one and all.*
Is there anything further that you'd like to say?

"That's all of the story that I'm willing to tell.
So I wish you Good Health and I bid you Good Day."

Nighttime

Tonight black Shadow steals abroad.
He stalks the sleeping neighborhood,
A spirit apart and not apart.
The stars and poplars stand alert;
A pausing moment stills the breezes;
The moon its mooniness increases.

Midnight smothers the day's disorder.
Shadow crouches in the flower border,
Unseen, unseeable as the night,
Until a wayward Ford headlight
Strikes him suddenly with its glare
To ignite his eyes with emerald fire,
And in that startling instant display
A Personage concealed by day.

Morris

The chair she sat in with an earnest groan
Was lumpy, frumpy, boggy, saggy, butt
Sprung and dingy, weary to the bone,
And older than the pleasures of King Tut.

Where it came from no one now recalled;
It was so long a part of Family
No one noticed how it had grown bald
And spavined, unsteady as Uncle McGhee.

Our aunt would sit there like she owned the place,
And yet she seemed a property of the chair,
As beauty is a property of grace,
Right angles the properties of a square.

Now Aunt Edna's gone. The chair remains,
With drowsy Audrey nestled in its warm
Complacent cushions with their ancient stains
And mends and redolent maternal charm.

It comforts her as it has comforted
Two generations of kin and eight of cats.
No longer proud, its noblest glories fled,
It humbly embraces kerchiefs and hats.

Morris Revisited

Now Audrey wakes, departs the chair,
And darts away to seek her mom
And inquire where the cookies are.
Brewster, with accustomed aplomb,
Deserts his corner, crosses the room,
And bounds onto the cushion where
Audrey has left a warm impression.

Three times he turns, then settles down;
Beneath his chest he tucks black paws;
Enjoys a silent, resounding yawn,
Curls his tail round to guard his nose.
This Chair is the finest that Nature affords:
He doesn't confide his thought in words.
We divine it from his expression.

Window Seat

Out of the spaces water drips or plummets.
Green fountains surge and brandish their tall blather.
The sky's pale pillows buff against each other.
Birds whistle endlessly from dizzy summits.

Small people growl along in loud cocoons
Or stroll with savages tied to their hands.
The morning sun at the world's rim expands;
At night divides itself into sparkling moons.

The cocoon honks bounce loudly off the pane,
But squeals of braggart blue jays pierce straight through.
The fountains fling their umber shreds a-strew
And now the dripping water drops again.

And now the dripping changes into white
And everything out there grows plump and mute
And wind sounds in the chimney its cool hoot.
The moon's slow drifting silvers the long night . . .

Outside is merely pictures. Reality
Is here: food bowl, throw rug, and litter box,
Chair legs, the steady tocking of the clocks,
The funky laundry hamper, the TV.

Yet Chloe's hypnotized by the exterior.
Time after time, perhaps against her will,
She crouches twitching on the window sill.
—Reality's a comfort, but Art is superior.

Solo Cello

This pleasant room throbs with a warm vibrato
that swarms the air from everywhere, nowhere.
Then you discover that *Claudia dozes,* indrawn
and safe, *supremely at peace* with all the world that is
and isn't, *on Barbara's knees.* She tucks her paws
beneath her. *One eye closes,* but not in sleep,
not yet; *the other sees,* through a haze of drowse,
a bowl of roses on the antique sideboard
and through the window *the shadow of trees* moonlit.

And all these things are known and in her power
and each and all enfolded within her purr.

Duet

But what is the source of the delicate ostinato
that accompanies the ground with a gentle air?
Listen . . . *In this cozy lull,* as night comes on,
Aunt Barbara's snore, amiable as a breeze,
is so light and pure, so consonant with the laws
of counterpoint, *she's unaware,* asleep,
that with the purr of Claudia in her wooze
it harmonizes, as if slyly scored
by Schubert. *The night is full* of trees and moonlight;
Aunt Barbara's world is full *of small surprises.*

As we tiptoe away and leave them there,
Claudia will know that we were here.

Tails

Contentment

In the late, last glow the hearth fire throws
Eugie sinks deeply into her doze,
Nodding her tail tip lazily:
      One   two   three.
Sometimes, unknowing, she adds one more:
      One   two   three   four.

Stupor

Floating down
To the darkest zone,
Now and then
She crooks the tip.

No telling when.

Oscillation

Slowly she paces across the lawn.
Her tail extends the graceful line
Of the easy sine wave of her spine.

Inspection

Sidling through the hallway door,
She advances to our visitor,
Sniffs his ankles and his clogs.
This guy hangs out with two dogs.

The inspection continues until at last
With tail held tall as a schooner mast,
She rejects encounter with a practiced sneer.
So long, Jack. I'm outta here.

Envelopment

Babushka's tail
Is a useful veil
She often plies
Around her eyes
To fend away
The light of day
Where she lies curled
In her small, warm world,
Secure from the strife
Of daily life
And its infinite grief.

Babushka, sleep well.

Thank you, Tail.

Odalisque

Ayesha disposes her languid form
Upon, among, within the shawls
And scarves and lengths of levantine
Matisse has strewn on her divan,
Insouciant arabesques and tourbillons
Of joyful color. There she lies,
Her coat as dark as the dark of the moon,
Her chest-blaze white, her eyes topaz,
The parti-hued, seductive tail,
Guidon of amorous temperament
And piquant personality,
Nowhere to be seen, hélas!

Cher maître Henri folds it into
His vision of the larger design
And the provocative Ayesha

Becomes but a decorative element
Like the bowl of vibrant roses,
No longer able to corrupt
Even the lowliest embassy clerk.

Little by Little

The symptoms of the aging Sparky include
          Painful arthritis,
        A touch of bursitis,
  A pronounced distaste for healthy food.
Tedious for him to sit or rise:
He curls his tail in a sturdy bow,
Then slowly centers it below
    His anus. When that is done,
He lowers his haunches one by one
And when he feels secure and sound
Settles Sparky upon the ground.

This I have observed with my own eyes.

Majesty

Caesar bears a tail
That all must hail.
The brush so full and fine
Is a marvel of design;
The length is truly superior
And ennobles his posterior.
When he trolls it under the moon
All the pusses swoon
And take a great delight
In teasing it all night.

Daily he gives thanks
     He's not a Manx.

Rondo

What followeth me passionately I pursue;
Whirled in a maelstrom of wild energy,
As subject and as object, I hurtle to
    What followeth me.

Although the chase be futile, inevitably
I find myself pursuing, each time anew,
What I possess that ever doth me flee.

I wind up doing what I abhor to do;
I wind and wind and wind, till dizzily
I fail to capture, as I adore to do,
    What followeth me.

New Year's Eve

Slyboots slides through Smugglers Wood
Overlooking Morgantown,
Then perches on the hill to spy
Whatever may be going on
In every noisy neighborhood
Of his small, uptight, middle-class city
While the sober stars peer down.

Then he steals along the trail
That brings him into Pembroke Park
Where chilly, fumbling lovers sigh
Eternal vows that shall not fail
Until the sun shoos off the dark.
The fox he eludes, the police patrol,
And the attentive, insomniac owl.

He trots the bike-path by Greene River,
And Chandlers Lane he scurries through,
To lose himself in the neon welter
And raucous rock of Broad Avenue
With the bootleg catnip he'll deliver
To his luckless pals in the Animal Shelter.

Time Piece

1

In the putative desert Mouse flings a Brick
high into the air.
A rubber cactus observes without comment.

The lone and level sands stretch far away.

2

Mouse winds a Clock and places it
upon a hummock.
He stares at it with fixed concentration as the sun
goes down behind a house or perhaps a teapot.

3

Nightfall delivers a moon like a melon slice.
Kop and Krazy appear and stand and stare
alongside Mouse upon the indifferent Clock
in meditative silence.

4

Kop and Mouse and Krazy still observe
the taciturn Clock. Morning comes and sparse birds
enliven the sky above a tenement or maybe
a red stone cliff.

5

Clock ringrings and Brick descends
to Pow! the brain of Krazy into heppy little hearts
that dance about the head. Mouse flees. Kop pursues.
"O such blessid messij from my Ignatz!"

6

Without a cactus a desert is only a plain.
The business of a Mouse is Mischief.
A Kop is always bulkier than you and me.
Love is not love that heaves no timely brick.
The landscape changes and our roles do not.
Always to be heppy is to be Krazy.

Dark Star

Black Stella in the patio
Absorbs so greedily the light
She alters the precarious ratio
Of energies that pulse in it,
As she diminishes bit by bit
The sun that once held back the night.

For she is the companion star,
Small but of such density
Our daily Sol must orbit her.
She siphons his immensity
At such a pace that all too soon
He'll shrivel to a wrinkled prune
And gild no more the harvest moon.

The Acrophile

Topper toes to the leafy tip
Of the elm of Thelma Blankenship.

There he settles to survey
The bourgeois doings of the day;

Tammi Johnson's Cadillac
Rolls to the soccer field and back;

Rhonda Johnson scours and mops,
One eye on the TV soaps;

Joe Bob hammers at Debussy,
Stopping often to go and pee;

Clanging into her cluttered garage
Pulls dear, near-sighted Mrs. Hodge;

Herman Rankin's handsome collie
Indulges in an amorous folly;

And now the husbands homeward come
Ho hum ho hum ho hum ho hum.

Topper sees nothing to interest
A blasé feline in the least;

Then, as he readies to desert his limb,
The firemen arrive to rescue him.

The Burrower

But Scaredycat may be part mole,
The way she paws a cozy hole

Under a cushion or a shawl
Or behind the drape that shrouds a wall.

The leastest vacancy in a shelf
Provides a space to hide herself,

And when no better locale can suit,
She seeks an occupiable boot.

During a thunderstorm we saw her
Peeking from a linen drawer,

And when frost beards the windowpane
She snuggles beneath the counterpane,

A molded, dreaming, humble mound
That does not stir or make a sound:

Then it is most pleasing to see
Her invisibility.

Lady Graye

The cat comes in on little fog feet.
　　　　How does a creature so small
Occupy this silent parlor
　　　　From wall to wall?

Presence

Silence came into the room;
Sat; and folded his paws beneath.
After an hour he moved along
And the emptiness regained its breath.

White Out

Longhair Silkie disposes what she is
Upon the window sill
To watch the breathless snow
Take apart the heavy sky
And let the pieces fall,
Subduing Landro Hill
And Shepherd Road where no one passes by.

Serene sisters, Silkie and the snow.
She obeys the vow of silence
That enrobes her mind
As the mindless snowfall
Mantles the blind land.
Her coat is as white as the mind
That listens to the sound the wind
Never makes at all.

Snow.   Snow.
The world absorbs her stare.
Anywhere is everywhere.
Silkie is at one with the universe
No longer there.

The Animals of Heaven

How shall they find us in that world beyond,
Where all is alien to the one we've known?
Will we retain the forms to which they bond
In present time, or different shapes put on?

Imagine us in that Hereafter Place
Where we have changed into another race
Of beings, no longer clumsy and afraid,
Neglectful, purblind, and self-satisfied,
So many times harmful by accident,
Or, at our worst, cruel by intent.

There they await us, hoping to recognize
The friends they honored for our nicer halves.
We never saw, not seeing through their eyes,
They loved us better than we loved ourselves.

CPSIA information can be obtained at www.ICGtesting.com
Printed in the USA
BVOW07s2329040914

365406BV00001B/14/P